THE BEST STRATEGIES FOR BUILDING CASH

HOW TO EARN A SOLID INCOME ONLINE

TABLE OF CONTENTS

Introduction 3
Busting Out The Myths 3-5
Getting Started 5-7
Types Of Legitimate Online Businesses 7
    Service Based Businesses 7-9
    Affiliate Marketing 9-10
        Selling On eBay 11-12
        Making Money From Membership Sites 12-13
        Making Money From Selling Products 13-15
        Make Money The PLR Way 15-16
        Make Money From Selling Informational Type Products 16-18
        Make Money Blogging 18-20
        Make Money Coaching Others 20-21
        Make Money In The Genealogy Business 21-22
        Make Money With Desktop Publishing 23-24
    Creating A Business From Unusual Ideas 24
Marketing Your Online Businesses 25
    Website 25-26
    Email Marketing 26-27
    Articles & Other Written Content 27-28
    Socializing For Marketing 28
    Miscellaneous Marketing Techniques 29-30
Marketing On The Fun Side 30
Ending Thoughts 31

Cash Building Strategies
How to Earn a Solid Income Online

We live in an uncertain world, but there is one thing we do know that is certain… and that is that times are tough. Inflation is rising on pretty much all fronts. You're busting your tail to make ends meet, but just when you think you're making some head way; Life throws a curve ball at you that strikes you out at home plate.

Bills are piling up, the cost of necessities is rising and gas prices continue to fluctuate. You have met a time in your life that working for a living seems to be shoving you further in a hole you can't dig out of.

Take a Deep Breath… Relax … and review the following report as this will help you realize there is an answer to this maddening situation you have found yourself in. You can earn a living that doesn't bury you like an avalanche. You can rise up and see the soul-warming sunshine that others have seen.

Take comfort in knowing that inner peace is at your grasp; and we'll show you how to find it by obtaining your income online.

Busting Out the Myths

Since we're talking about earning a living online; it's important that the issues of internet fraud be addressed. You want to be aware, but there's no reason to let doubt get in your way when deciding the online business path you should take.

Scams, spam and fraud seem to synonymous with the word internet these days. So many cynics put this way of earning a living down, just because the internet is involved. They will yell scam or fraud on the rooftops upon hearing any kind of online money-making opportunity.

While there are scams out there in the online business cyberspace, there are just as many legitimate opportunities to explore. Researching will bring you a lot of information and tips to spotting these scams, so you can move forward- to earning a living from the comfort of your own home.

Over the years, scams and fraud have grown in all areas of the internet, which have made people, understandably, concerned of doing anything online. There are legitimate ways to make your money on the internet - a lot of people have successfully done so and continue to do so today. So, don't let this opportunity pass you by, because of lingering doubts.

This report will show you how you can make the money legitimately and avoid those nasty scams that could prey on you.

The more informed you are about internet scams, the more confident you will be when searching for an online business. Take the upper hand and be in control of your business future before someone tries to take advantage of you. Let's bust some of the scam myths!

Here are some of the popular statements made by most of the internet frauds and the truth behind them:

Myth- *"Make Money Overnight!"* – These scams promise you a way of making money while you sleep. They make it sound like there is little work involved to obtaining this.

Truth- While it's certainly possible to achieve, it will take hard work and much dedication to be able to make this claim. Most online businesses will take a little time to get up and running, but will be worth your effort in the end.

Myth- *"Turn your Computer into a Money making cash machine!"*- Actually, there are a lot of statements that start off with this kind of sales pitch.

Truth- The statement itself could be true, but be careful of a sales pitch that starts off this way. Most online business opportunities sell the business itself. Scammers tend to sell the money making benefit. Usually, in that case, there really is no business- to you that is. To the scammer they're making money off people paying them for what they say they will give you.

Myth- *"Start your business absolutely free- No money involved!"*- They push the fact that you can get a business going with absolutely no money in start -up fees.

Truth-This type of scam will scream the 'no money involved' statement, but then turn around and ask you to pay them a certain amount for information on how to get a business started for free. Hmm…. Aren't they contradicting themselves? There will be some costs to start up a business, but very rarely do they ever break the bank.

Myth- *"Start Earning a Living from Typing at Home"*- This statement is similar to a lot of others plastered on the internet claiming that you can start a business from home with your typing or in some cases, data entry skills.

Truth- Yes, you can earn money typing or performing data entry from home, but not with guys. You're better off offering these services to clients yourself and avoid paying the scammers for

4

the information on how to do it. You can find out how to do it -with your own research for Free!

There are many more scam opportunities out there, but these will give you some ideas on how those frauds work and who they like to prey upon. Be aware of your options and don't be afraid to research any opportunity you don't feel comfortable with.

Getting Started

The fear of the getting started process tends to make people procrastinate in starting a business of their own. That fear usually boils down to the fact that they just don't know how to do it, or where to even start. This report will help you with this process, so you can lay your fears to rest and move through the getting started phase with ease.

Let's start with some commonly asked questions that most newbies have in the getting started process.

"Do I have to have special skills or degrees to start my own business?"

You will need to have some knowledge in the field you're going to embark in, but it's not necessary to have any business or college degrees to accomplish starting your own business. Of course, it will depend on the type of business you want to start.

Simple research in the field you're potential business will be in, will be sufficient enough to give you what you need in most cases. If you're planning to offer a service like web designing, etc; you should have some skills in that area before trying to start your business.

College degrees and experience are always helpful in gaining expertise in a field, but you usually don't have to have any degrees to have your own online business. Knowledge has more power online, so reading everything you can get your hands on that deals with your field will more important.

Will it Cost a lot of money?"

Starting your own online business doesn't generally cost much money. The money you put into it is mostly for a computer, internet access and a website. Any other costs will be based on the type of business you want to get into.

Businesses where you will sell items you've created, will take some money to stock the inventory items, but there are great deals on the internet to be found for this purpose. If you plan to sell a service, like web designing, software programs will need to be added to your list of tools to purchase.

For the most part, you won't have to run to your local bank and beg them to offer you a loan. Find the best deals on the items you need for the business you choose and you won't have to worry about the interest rates a loan would add to your budget.

"Will I still be able to start my own business online, even if I've never run my own business before?"

Absolutely. Hundreds of Internet Marketers have started their own businesses and made a success of it without having any previous business experience. Again, it all adds up to how much time and effort you put into your research.

The internet, itself, holds a plethora of information at your fingertips to help you learn every aspect of the business you want to start. You can find tips, tricks and all sorts of information from people who've been there and done it, so utilize this resource to gain the power that knowledge will bring you.

"How much money can I make from an online business?"

This will vary on a lot of factors. What business you start, how much time and effort you put into it and the return of investment on what you're offering; all play a part in what you will essentially make.

Some internet marketers make a six figure income, while others make the same amount a full time fast food worker generally makes. No matter how much your business brings in, you will still be ahead of those who commute to their jobs. The money they spend on gas, clothes for work and meals etc; is money that goes into your pocket and not someone else's.

"Do I really need a website?"

A website will be needed to conduct your business from. You will need to sell your products or show potential clients what services you have to offer. It serves as your 'office' or 'store' would, only you won't need to rent out expensive space in a building to use for your online business.

Websites are pretty easy to create if you use one of the many website design software programs or website building services. If you choose to, you can also hire a web designer to create a killer site for your business, so don't let your lack of web designing skills hold you back.

"Do I need special business licenses to run an online business?"

You will want to check with your local government agencies to determine what you will need in your area. Each area is different, so it's best to check and see what you need before starting your business.

"I'm nervous about taking money from customers. What if I mess up the payment processing system?"

If you're selling items, you will want to use an online payment system like PayPal or Clickbank. These programs will take of the whole payment process for you including refunds. Shopping cart software a lot of times will come with a web building program, so take advantage of that option.

Types of Legitimate Online Businesses

There are several types of online businesses you can choose from to get started. You will want to check out each option and see which one suits your needs before proceeding. Here are some of the more popular online businesses people get into and what each one entails:

Service Based Businesses

A service based business is one where you offer some type of service to potential clients. Some of these include:

Writing

Web Design

Accounting/Bookkeeping

Virtual Assistant

Other small business owners have a tough time getting all of their business tasks done by themsleves, so they outsource those projects to someone else. They look for people who offer the services they need done for them.

If you have experience in some of these areas, you could offer it as a service by starting your own business selling yourself. For example, if you have some writing experience and can write well, you can offer that as a service to others who need writing done for their sites.

What skills are needed?

Depending on the type of service you choose to provide your potential clients, you should have some amount of skill under your belt. It's not necessary to have educational degrees to perform these services, but clients like to see that you have some kind of experience to complete the tasks they need done.

Working online doesn't provide the face to face contact that brick and mortar companies have when they hire employees. Trust comes a little harder online, so people do like to know the person they're hiring has skills and knowledge in a particular field.

While it's not necessary to have 10+ years experience performing a service, the fact that you have done it before and have some testimonials to back that claim up helps tremendously.

What tools are needed?

The tools you need will depend on the type of services you plan to provide. The more common ones that most service based businesses should have are:

Computer

Reliable Internet access

Phone

E-mail program

Website

There will probably be some software programs to obtain as well. Each service uses some different ones, but most need a word processing program, excel program, and some use a web designing program.

You should consider an Instant Messaging program for those clients who like to be able to contact you instantly without having to use the phone to call or wait for an e-mail response.

How do you get started?

First thing you want to do is decide on the type of service you plan to offer your clients. Jot down everything you can think of that shows you have some experience or knowledge in that particular field.

Next, get your website created. Showcase your skills or experience on your site and provide clients with testimonials from other people who have used your skills and were pleased with the results. Place your rates and any other information about how you run your business.

Market your site on various places on the internet to get your online business out there for potential clients to find and check out. When clients contact you to hire you for whatever service they need, reiterate to them how things will go. For example, let them know how they be invoiced for the work done and how much it will cost etc.
It will take awhile to build a list of regular clients, so don't expect to be making tons of money right away. Give it time and keep marketing your service based business until you get to the point where you're practically turning away clients because you're too busy.

Running a service based business is a perfect option for those who already are performing that service at another job. In most cases, you could make more money offering those services online than you can by working a brick and mortar position.

Affiliate Marketing

This is an online business where you use your selling and marketing expertise to get consumers to buy other people's products and earn income from the sale you made. Typically, you would earn a pre-determined amount of money based on the sales you make of those products, but in some cases, you could make money from the clicks from your site that get the consumers to the affiliate websites.

Sometimes you can earn money by getting customers to sign up for things on the affiliate sites, such as newsletters etc. Each affiliate program will discuss this further on how they work, so when you sign up for their program, be sure to check out how their process works. This will be kept track of through an affiliate link that you're provided with to place on your site.
What skills are helpful?

You don't have to be a salesman or a marketer to be an affiliate marketer. Knowledge on how to do these things will be important though. Learn everything you can about how online marketing works and learn how to be a successful affiliate marketer from other top marketers.

It will take hard work and much dedication to get your affiliate marketing business to be a successful one. If you don't have the time nor the gumption to work hard, don't consider this to be your online business.

What tools are needed?

The tools needed will be minimal. Besides the usual computer with reliable internet access, you will need a website to sell the affiliate products from. You won't have to stock up on the products, just to sell them.

Your website will need fresh content on a regular basis, so be prepared to either write some articles yourself or hire someone to do them for you. A blog to link to your site will be helpful as well to make the search engines happy with you.

How do you get started?

You will need to determine what niche you have for your affiliate marketing website. This helps you to stand out from your competitors. For example, you could use nutrition as your niche. Then create a website based on the niche you chose for your business.

Then find affiliate products to sell from that site. Make sure that the products you decide to sell for your business are related in some way to the niche you have chosen for your affiliate marketing business.

So, if your niche is in the nutritional field, you will want to offer affiliate products that are related in some way to nutrition. If you don't offer related products in your business, you run the risk of appearing as unprofessional and the search engines won't be too pleased with you as well.

There are many people who make quite a bit of money running this type of business. It's important to remember that the most work you will have in this type of business will be marketing your website to get consumers to find you. When they find you, your site should be able to get them interested in your products to the point where they will buy using your links.

Selling on E-Bay

This is another popular online business that a lot of people usually start out with. E-Bay is a popular online auction website that millions of people use every day to find good deals on items they are looking for.

You can sell anything you have at home as well as selling items using a drop ship method. If you do a search on the e-bay site, you will see a whole variety of items that people are selling. They could be used items or brand new items that come from wholesalers. Either way, people will pay good money if you provide them with what they're looking for.

Some people go so far as to buy items from flea markets and garage sales for the sole purpose of reselling them on e-bay for a profit.

What skills are helpful?

There aren't a lot of skills you would need to sell items on e-bay. The ability to market your items will be the most important one to have. People can do a search on the site for the items you're selling, but if you want to make money in this type of business, you will want to market those items elsewhere to get people to find them.

If you're selling items from your home, you should be able to take a good photo of the item so people can see what shape the item is in.

What tools are needed?

Really, the only tools you should need to start this type of business is an account with e-bay to sell your items. If you plan to use a drop ship method, you would have to find a wholesaler that will ship the items direct to the customers.

An access to a computer with a reliable internet access will be necessary to keep track of your sales. You will also need an online account like PayPal to receive money from your customers.

How do you get started?

Sign up for an account with E-Bay that allows you to sell from them. Plan to purchase items from the site as well to help build your user ratings, so people will have a little more confidence in buying from you.

Place photos, if possible, of the items that you want to sell. Items that have a photo of items sell much faster than those that don't. People like to see what it is they're buying, so provide them with the best quality photo possible.

Review all informational materials as well as the rules on the E-Bay website, to get tips on making more sales and how the process of selling on the site works.

Selling on E-Bay is an excellent way to start your own online business. This gives you your first taste of an online business without having to have a lot of equipment to get you started. Plus, you get the benefit of getting rid of items that are cluttering up your home while you make a little money on the side.

Making money from Membership Sites

Some online business owners make money from selling memberships to their websites. People purchase memberships to gain access to content that the website owner provides them on a regular basis.

For example, you may offer memberships to internet users who are need of articles for their websites. The memberships would need to be renewed every few months or so depending on how long your memberships are good for. Every time someone renews their membership, you make more money.

The profit potential for this kind of business is pretty high. It won't cost much to provide your members with informational items, but you could charge them a nice amount to access them, giving you a profit that keeps on giving.

What skills are helpful?

Marketing skills will be the most helpful. Getting those internet users to your site to purchase your memberships is what will make you the money. Having some knowledge of running a website could be useful as well to keep your site running smoothly for your members.

You may want to have some knowledge of the products you're offering. For example, if you're offering articles to your members, you should know what makes a good article and how they work for the different purposes.

What tools are needed?

You will need a high quality website to handle the demands that membership site will bring. There should provide excellent service should something go wrong with the site. There are some membership site management software programs that can help you get one set up and running for less than $100.

Content for the site is another tool you will need. You need to provide your paying members with fresh content to use regularly. It could be in the form of written articles, software programs or even online games, depending on what you plan to give your members.

How do you get started?

You will need to plan your membership site beforehand. What do you plan to offer your members? Will it be content, software etc? When you have made your decision, then come up with a new and different angle to provide your consumers.

You could provide content in a specific niche, like nutrition or you could offer a certain kind of written content-whatever it takes to get provide internet users with a fresh angle. This helps you stand out from the crowd of competitors out there.

Next, get your membership site created with a shopping cart feature to handle the payments for the memberships. The membership management software programs should come with all you need to accomplish your business. All you would then need is the content to give to your members.

The most important step will be to market your membership site to get people to find you. Marketing techniques will be discussed later on in this report.

Membership sites can offer you a means of earning residual type income. If people are satisfied with what you give them, they will have no problems handing you their money to keep renewing their access to your site's content.

Making Money From Selling Products

This type of business can be done in a few different ways. One way is to create and sell your own products. Crafters often get into this type of business to sell their own creations to the internet public. Scrapbook creators also choose this path for their business.

Another way to sell products is by using an online store selling other products. There would be no inventory of items to stock in your home, nor do you have to ship anything directly from your own location. The products are ordered through the 'store' you have set up and the wholesaler providing the products will ship the items direct to the customers for you.

What skills are helpful?

The skills you should have are the ability for hard work and good customer service skills. A lot of your time will be spent marketing your websites, so potential customers will find you. Having a good website set up will be necessary to provide the customers will everything they need when deciding whether or not to buy your products.

Customers will have questions about the products and may have some problems that you will need to address, so good customer service skills will be a must. Establishing good rapport with your customer will start the cycle going of them coming back to buy more from you. Providing them with top notch customer service will help you gain that.

What tools are needed?

If you have chosen to sell products that you create yourself; you will need to stock up on an inventory of items to create them. Check with some vendors to find good deals on items that are purchased in bulk to help you save some money.

Of course a website will be necessary as well as your customers will need to find your products, see what they are and have a way to order what you're offering. Make sure the site has the shopping cart feature to make the purchasing process easier for your business.

How do you get started?

The first thing you will want to do is to decide what you're going to sell. Are you creating your own products to offer or are you planning to sell other products through the use of drop shippers?

If you're planning to sell items you create yourself, then you will need to research vendors for the inventory you will need to make those products. Have some made up ahead of time, so that when consumers start to order your product, you can ship them out right away and not make them wait another day or two while you make them up.

When the planning stage is done, you will need to get your website created to sell them from. Make sure the site is easy to navigate and isn't so distracting that they get turned off from your business within a few seconds.

Of course, the last step in getting started in this business will be marketing your products, which will be discussed further on in this report. This step is the most important one if you want your business to be a success, so don't skimp on this one.

Selling products is an excellent way to make some money online. If you already create products to give away as gifts to friends and family, there's no reason why you shouldn't take the product to the internet and start selling them.

If you like the idea of selling products, but don't want to create one to make yourself or if you just don't feel you are creative then you can still achieve this kind of business by having someone else ship products for you. Getting started this way online gives you the flexibility to spend the time needed with your family, but still earn a living.

Making money the PLR way

PLR stands for Paid Label Rights. Its written content that can be sold to others to use for whatever they want to use it for. Website owners search these out to get content for their sites for a smaller fee.

It doesn't sound like a money making opportunity when put that way. The thing is, the same package of written content can be sold numerous times to other people. Here's how it works. For example, let's say you are selling a package of 10 articles- all about a certain topic like pet care. Typically, these packages are sold at about $1 an article. Someone who has a website about pet care needs articles to place on their site, so they buy a package from you. You just made $10.

Now, that same package of 10 articles can be sold again and again and again. In the end, you can sell the same 10 articles 50 times bringing you the grand total of $500 just for that one package. You can sell more than one package of PLR articles at the same time increasing your profit potential.

Everyone charges something different and offers different types of PLR content as well as different article topics. You can sell E-book material and special reports as well as articles. People can take these articles, change them to their needs and use them wherever they want.

What skills are helpful?

Writing skills would be necessary. You would need to write good quality articles even though the people that buy them will change them anyway. You could hire a ghostwriter to write them for, but keep in mind; you would have to pay them for their time, so this is a good option if you don't mind losing some of the profit.

Marketing your PLR content would also be necessary. In order to make good money in this business, you will need to get people to find your content, so pull out all the stops when starting this business.

What tools will I need?

If you're going to write the article content yourself, you would need a computer with word processing software installed. A website will also be needed to sell your PLR content from.

If you choose to hire someone to write the content for you, then you will need to find a ghostwriter that fits your budget and provides good quality content.

How do you get started?

The first place to start will be in getting the articles written. You will want to make sure that the package of articles that you will sell together relate to a certain topic. Topics could include gardening, pet care, nutrition, exercise etc.

Decide how much you will sell the articles for and get a website set up to sell them from. You can certainly use a website that provides the service of selling them for you, but you're better off selling them off your own site and marketing them yourself.

There is good money in PLR if you choose to get into this kind of business, as there are millions of websites out there that need content. With good marketing techniques, you can make a good living for you and your family quite easily.

Make Money From Selling Informational Type Products

The internet is a great place to sell your knowledge. There are many people who will pay almost anything to get information they're desperately looking for. If you have the knowledge that they want, you could earn a substantial income.

Informational products come in many forms. It could be one of the following:

- E-Books
- E-Courses
- Tutorials

Guides

Podcasts

These are popular informational products that are well sought after by internet users all over. If you have something to say, this could be the business for you.
What skills are helpful?

You should have knowledge of the topic that you're going to present to your consumers. It won't be necessary to have a doctorate degree or of any kind to do this, but having a good amount of knowledge in the field would be helpful.

The ability to market your materials will also be helpful. The more people you reach with your products, the more people who may want to buy from you.
What Tools will be needed?

The tools you need will depend on what you plan to provide. E-Books and Guides could be written on word processing software and then converted to a PDF document, which is the most popular type of document people want.

Autoresponder programs will be needed for creating successful e-courses. Podcasts would need audio recording and editing software. Tutorials could be done a couple of different ways. You could use a power point presentation to present you material or you could use video tutorial software. Video tutorials are great for showing users how to use a specific program step by step.

Websites and blogs will be necessary to promote your informational products from as well.

How to get started

You will need to decide on a topic for your product. What do you have the most knowledge about that you could provide your potential consumers? When you know what you want to provide, then research that topic to see if you can find a new and unique angle to present it in.

Since there are lots of E-Books, tutorials etc. on the internet for sale, you will need to find something new to give to your customers. They won't be as willing to hand over their money if they don't think you have something new to give them.

Write out or record your informational product and then edit them to your satisfaction. Once you have it the way you want it, then you can start selling it. Create a blog or website to sell it from and make sure the site's web copy content grabs internet user's attention so they can purchase what you're offering.

Hire a copywriter if you can afford one to write the copy to promote those materials. They can write content in a way that makes your product so desirable that anyone would want to purchase it.

Creating informational products won't cost you much, but you can sell them for a nice profit. This is an excellent way to earn income online while maintaining a flexible schedule which allows you to spend more time with your family.

Make Money Blogging

Blogging started out years ago as a way for people to connect to others and share pictures, stories and experiences. It was considered to be a great personal journal type tool that one could use to leave their mark on the internet through their encounters.

Blogs then evolved to become excellent Marketing Tools as well as a medium to make money off of. There are a few different ways to earn income from blogging. Here are a few:

Adsense ads- The popular search engines offer a way to earn a little extra money with any blog or website. The idea is to place these ads on your site and when a visitor clicks on an ad from your site, you earn a pre-determined amount of money. The more clicks you can get from your site visitors, the more you can make. There are some rules, so if you choose to go this route, be sure to learn what not to do before signing up for their programs.

Product Reviews- There are some websites that you can sign up with that can help you connect with other companies who need people to review their products and get them some exposure on your blogs. Usually the main requirement for this is to have a blog that's been around for awhile and has a fair amount of visitors. Those companies would pay you a specified amount to review their product on your blog.

Contextual Links- Some business or website owners will pay a blogger to post one of their links within their blog posts. It may be the owners themselves contacting the blog author or a company that acts as the middleman. Those businesses will find blogs that relate to their companies sites, so the links provided on the blogs will be search engine friendly. This is a great way to earn some extra traffic for a site.

Sell products- Blogs are another way you can sell your own products from. Those who have businesses selling home décor items or food container items use blogs a lot to help sell their products and make more money online.

What skills would be helpful?

There isn't much skill involved in this type of business except the ability to market your blog. You would want to research blogging as much as possible to learn some of the tricks of the trade to get your blog popular.

What Tools would be needed?

Your main tool, besides a computer with an internet connection, would be a blog. There are many blogging programs out there to choose from. Some are free to set up with, while others require a monthly or annual fee to get started with.

The paid versions of blogging programs can help you connect with other blogs and increase your blog's traffic. The free versions are extremely easy to set up and most are extremely popular amongst bloggers, so finding people to connect with wouldn't be too hard to do.

How to get started

Sign up with a blogging program and start posting entries to it. Make sure you're blogging on a regular basis, which would be about 2 times a week. Blogs that aren't updated regularly tend to get lost in cyberspace.

Market your blog as much as possible. Get listed on blog directories, get on other people's blog rolls and comment on other blog author's posts to get some exposure to your blog. The more traffic you can drive to your blog, the higher your chance of making blogging a lucrative way to make money.

Most of the blogging programs will have a sign up for adsense ads already included in their set up feature, so getting started with that will be easy. If you want to provide product reviews and contextual links, you will want to be blogging for awhile and have a fair amount of traffic coming to it.

When your blog is ready, find the companies that will help you connect with businesses that want to pay to have their products reviewed or have their links embedded with your blog post entries. Once that's set up, you can start earning some extra income with your blog.

Blogging is an easy way to earn some extra cash if you plan to work hard at marketing it. The ones successful at blogging for money use every route possible to get their blog well known in the internet communities. The ones that don't, tend to earn only a few cents a week.

Become one of the more successful bloggers and make your blog your business and not just a hobby to partake in once in awhile. Your pocketbook will thank you for it.

Making Money Coaching Others

A coach is one who takes their know-how in a particular craft and sharing it with others who want to be successful in that field as well. Coaches can be experts in anything from writing to marketing to business itself.

If you have good knowledge or experience in a particular area you can become a coach quite easily and make money doing it. There are many coaches who help others in web design, graphic design and even in the coaching field as well.

A coach would offer tips and techniques to newbies within that field and answer questions throughout their learning process.

What skills are helpful?

The most important skill you should have for this type of business is the ability to be a good listener. You should also have great patience for your clients. Those who hire you to coach them want you to listen to their bad experiences and help guide them out of the muck they find themselves in no matter how strange they may sound.

To build rapport and credibility in this business, you should know your field well. If you've never designed a website before, then being a web designing coach would not be a good idea, because your lack of experience will be spotted right away and trust will be lost.

What Tools will be needed?

You should have the following in this kind of business:

   Computer

   E-Mail program

   Website

- Informative content for your site
- Shopping cart feature for your site to handle payments
- Telephone dedicated for business purposes

Most of your conversations with clients will probably be through your e-mail programs, but some people may be more comfortable being able to talk to you on a more one on one basis, so a phone should be included in your list of tools.

How to get started

Plan your business out. What service will you be offering that you have knowledge in? Get some articles and other written content created to place on a website to help build credibility and expert status for your business.

Explain on your site how your service works and how much your rate will be. Show some testimonials from others who have used your services before and were pleased with the results. Make your site easily navigated so others won't get lost trying to find information about your coaching business.

Market your coaching business to get clients to come to you. Plan the goals that the client wants to achieve by using you and discuss how those goals will be obtained. Listen to their problems and questions and provide insightful answers and support to keep them moving forward to their goals.

Coaches are well sought after online for those who have good knowledge or experience in a certain area. Use what you know about a topic and provide a coaching service to others to help them become an expert like you in the same field.

Make Money in the Genealogy Business

This is a perfect business opportunity for those who love to research and love to learn about our ancestors. Genealogists make a living by creating family trees for other people who don't have the time or the patience to do it themselves.

Almost everyone likes to know where they came from and what their ancestors did that might have made a mark on the world. You can cash into their curiosities by doing the research for them and providing them with their family heritage.

What skills would be helpful?

Excellent research skills and organization skills will be of high priority. These skills are what genealogy is all about. You will need to know where and how to research each family's heritage and be able to place all the information in an easy to understand format for your clients.

What Tools would be needed?

You would need a computer with a reliable internet connection. You should subscribe to some of the best genealogy websites available to use for your research. You should also invest in some guides or attend some classes to learn some tips and tricks on researching family trees.

A website would be needed to run your business from. Clients will need to know how you perform you work as well as how much you charge. Provide some samples if possible to show clients how thorough your work is.

How to get started

Get all your supplies brought together and find genealogy websites to subscribe to. Create a website to sell your service from and then start marketing your business to get clients to your site.

Utilize your internet resources for your research as well as local libraries, courthouses and historical societies. You may need to interview people to access some information, so you may need to look into a phone to use.

Create your family tree document that will hold all the family heritage information or use software programs that provide that for you.

If you love to research and are interested in historical documents, then you should be considering this type of business. Meet the demands that people have to find out their family history and make money doing something you love to do.

Make Money with Desktop Publishing

If you're a creative person and can use a computer well, consider an online business with desktop publishing. This is where you create documents, flyers, brochures, calendars, and advertisements.

All these types of documents are created using a program or two from your computer, so having expensive machinery to create them will not be needed.

There are a lot of people looking for these creative pages for all kinds of uses and don't know how to create one themselves. If you have some knowledge in this area, you could use it to make money providing them with these creations.

What skills are helpful?

The ability to make your way around a computer and use various types of software programs are some skills you should have. You don't have to be an artist to be in this business, because everything is done using the computer.

What Tools are needed?

Besides a computer, you should have the following equipment:

- Desktop publishing software
- Photo editing software
- Laser or Color Printer
- Scanner
- High Quality printer paper

Make sure you know how to use all the features of your equipment well so you can provide the best quality service for your clients.

How to get started

You should obtain all the necessary equipment to run your business. Decide on a niche to target your marketing efforts to and then create a website to reflect that niche. Your website should provide potential clients with samples of your work to show your expertise in this field.

You could also brush up on your skills by reading any tutorials or guides about the desktop publishing field.

Desktop Publishing can be a very rewarding business for anyone to undertake who loves to achieve creations to make anyone envious. If you are one of those people and you want something that will provide flexibility, this is the business you should check into.

Creating a business from unusual ideas

We've discussed the more conventional means of starting an online business. There are some unconventional means as well that should be looked at. By unconventional, we mean those ideas that people came up and were laughed at by others. Those people than took those ideas to the top and made a huge living from them. Here are some of those ideas that people thought would never get off the ground:

Selling old seminars- One guy made a nice living by finding and selling old seminars that originally sold for thousands of dollars.

Domain names- Someone came up with the idea that they could sell a service of naming domain names for other people. Sounds crazy, but the business took off for them. Turns out quite a few people needed that service.

Selling used engagement jewelry- This idea reportedly came from someone who broke off their engagement, got the ring back but found they couldn't return it for full value. They started a site for other people in the same boat to sell their jewelry and earn back what they paid for it or as close to it as possible.

Selling butterflies for a living- Yes, it's possible or at least that what one person found out when someone bet him that he couldn't sell them. He not only won that bet, but made a huge business from that one little idea.

There are tons more ideas that people have come up and made them work as an online business, so check your memory banks and see if there's one idea hiding there that no one would believe could work. It just might prove them wrong...

Marketing Your Online Business Strategies to Make your Business Successful

Now that you've learned some different online businesses to choose from, you will want to learn some ways to market your business so it can become successful like many other internet marketers who have been down the path you want to travel.

Let's explore some of the more popular strategies of marketing your online business.

Website

Your online business website is the perfect place to start. If there's one thing that could make or break your business, it would be the website itself. Here are some things that are important to know about your website for marketing purposes:

Domain name- The domain name is the address to find your site on the internet. You want to choose a domain name that matches closely to your site or business name. This helps any internet user find your business easily if they're searching for a certain topic. An exact match would be the best option, but if it's not available, try finding one that comes as close as possible.

Keywords- Utilize the best keywords to place within the content on your site. Keywords are words that internet searchers use when they go to the search engines to find information on a specific topic. The keywords would get indexed by the search engine and placed within the results page for a user. The higher your site is ranked on the results page, the more chance you have that the user will choose your site to visit.

Market with a Niche- A niche narrows down your business to market to a certain group of people. Narrowing down your marketing efforts to a smaller group to help you give what your consumers want. Larger groups have too many people that have too many different needs. This makes it difficult to get your audience interested in what you have. The smaller groups will be the people that are more likely to want what you have, so marketing will be much easier.

Your website will need to reflect whatever niche you choose for your business. If you're targeting mothers with young children, your site should reflect that. You would have graphics that would connect to mothers with young children and the content on the site should be written to something they could relate to. This will help with the search engines as well.

Blog- Provide a blog to go with your website. It should relate to the theme your business site has. Personal blogs should not be used here. If you use a blogging program that isn't connected with your site, try to design the blog's template to match your business site as close as possible, so it appears that the blog goes along with the site.

Blogs are another way to utilize the search engines to gain visitors. When a visitor finds your blog, they can see that you have more information to offer them on that topic elsewhere on your website, so they can just click through on the link provided.

E-Mail Marketing

E-mails are essential to any marketing campaign. This is how you keep your business and products fresh in your potential customer's minds. Getting a visitor to your site is one thing, but getting them to remember you over the millions of other websites out there is a whole thing in itself; especially when they're interested in buying.

E-mails come at regular intervals to provide information to website visitors to help build credibility as well as get your business name in the forefront of their minds. This can be done in a couple of different ways. To get e-mail addresses to send your messages to, you will provide an opt-in email feature on your site so that people can sign up for updates on what you're offering or for more information.

Newsletters- These are used to provide small articles in topics that relate to your business. For example, if you sell vitamins and minerals, your newsletter can offer articles on alternative health practices, etc. to show how important your product is to them.

Newsletters can be sent to their e-mail inboxes with the introduction to an article and a link where they can go to your site to read the rest of the article. This enables users to become familiar with your site and makes it easier to remember you when they decide they want to buy something you're offering.

E-Courses- You can have a sign up feature on your site for visitors to use to learn the basics about a topic. If you're selling vitamin products, you can use an e-course to help teach your readers how to pick the best ones for different kinds of health problems.

E-courses are typically sent over a 5-7 day period and are often offered for free. This keeps your business name in their minds by reminding of it every day that the e-course comes into their inbox.

Updates- For those who have purchased something from you or people who have signed up for this feature, you can provide them with updates on your products, discounts, freebies, etc. This way if you don't hook a visitor into buying in their first visit they may see something later on that catches their eye and entices them to buy.

The updates can also help bring in more traffic for your site. Those who have already signed up for your lists will have friends, family, neighbors and co-workers that they could refer to your business by simply forwarding the messages on.

Articles and Other Written Content

Besides providing good website content, articles and other written content can be used in several ways to market your business. Here are some of those ways:

Articles directories- Article directories provide great marketing tactics to use for your business. By writing and submitting an article related to your business site, you can achieve two things...
1. Credibility in the topic you have written about

2. Drive more traffic to your site by providing a link to your business website in the author's bio section provided on the article directory sites.

These directory sites usually rank well with the search engine results page, so someone stumbling upon one of your articles submitted within a directory can find their way over to your website for more information on that topic.

Articles placed within other site's newsletters or blogs- By being a guest writer on someone else's blog or newsletter, you can reach a whole other group of people looking for information on one topic.

You would provide a link to your site within these articles and then reciprocate the favor for the other website owner to provide the same kind of articles on your newsletters or blogs.

Articles on Digg or similar sites- Having one of your articles submitted on Digg or a similar type site will gain you more access to your site. Digg is a site that provides articles other internet users have deemed as good informative articles. Those articles that receive a large number of "Diggs" will be pushed to the home page where a lot of users will see and review them. Your site link could be included for those people who want more information on the topic.

Offer E-books or Guides- These can provide your consumers with information on a topic while including a link back to your site to keep them familiar with your business. These can be offered for free or for a small fee.

The word Free can be a powerful word to any user and catch their attention quite easily. You would provide some basic information on a topic and could get them interested in buying an e-Book that has more in-depth information about the same topic.

Socializing for Marketing

One of the more successful ways to find traffic that are looking for what you have to offer is to socialize with others who are like-minded. Here are the most popular ways to socialize for your marketing needs:

Blogging comments- Find other blogs that have the same kind of topic as your website. Post a reply on some of their posts. Your website link will be associated with your name and those looking for more information on that topic will check out your site or blog and see what you have to offer them.

Join forum communities- Find message board communities that have topics that relate to your website. Your website link could go in the signature line allowing others to find their way to site to see what you have. Check with the rules of the board first to make sure this is allowed.

By posting regularly on these forums, you can build credibility as an expert for that topic and gain some trust with some potential consumers who may be thinking about buying from you. Also, the other board members may refer people they know to your site, so make sure you give back as much as you receive with these communities.

Social Networking Sites- Social networking sites include such popular sites like MySpace and Facebook. These sites attract people who are looking for others who are interested in the same things they are.

Internet marketers use them all the time to hook up with people in their target audience. People who have the same interest as you, can communicate and start to build trust with you. They will be more receptive to buy from someone who's in their "group" or they could pass on your business info. on to other people they know.

Miscellaneous Marketing Techniques

Here are some other techniques to utilize in your marketing campaigns:

Affiliate Programs- Start your affiliate programs for your products. Let other people earn some money by marketing your products for you. More traffic will find their way to your site through someone else's efforts.

Learn how to start your own successful affiliate program and create a web page on your site for others to sign up to be your affiliates. This is something that you can announce in your newsletters and update messages.

Adwords- Search engines offer this feature to Business owners to purchase advertising space on the search results pages. Every time someone clicks on that ad, you will be charged a certain amount of money to the search engine.

Because you're paying for the clicks, you will want to provide the most desirable ad possible to increase your return of investment. Poor ads can cost you money, because not everyone who clicks through these ads will want to buy. Keep track of these ads and pull them or revamp them when necessary to avoid losing too much money for your business.

Word of Mouth campaign- This is the easiest marketing technique there is. A simple word of mouth campaign will get people to pass on the information to your business to other people and so on.

This works great for local customers and clients to hear about your business and pass it on to others that may be looking for the same products or information. This is also an inexpensive way to accomplish marketing for your business.

Use Press Releases- This option can be used if you're just opening your doors or if you're offering a discount or special sale. Press Releases are submitted to sites that publish them for internet users who are looking for specific information.

They are written as if they're a news story and they showcase your "news" with eye catching and attention grabbing headlines and information. Your sale, discount or business startup would get plenty of exposure to potential consumers and clients.

A well written press release to announce what you are offering may just be what you need to drive a huge amount of traffic to your business website. Consider having one done on a period basis to help keep your business' name fresh on people's minds.

Place an ad in local papers- There's no rule that says you only have to market on the internet. Why not try marketing locally, by placing ads in local papers. Those advertisements are seen by most everyone that lives within that area and receives that paper.

Sometimes, businesses gain their first sales transactions from local customers, so don't leave out your local area when planning your marketing campaign.

Podcasting- Podcasting is audio content that people use to provide information that people listen to instead of read. It gives them a different medium to learn about a topic their interested in. People love the option of the podcast to listen to while they do something else and not have to be glued to their computer screen.

Your business gains credibility and trust amongst the listeners. Those listeners can become customers, so your website will be linked to the audio program.

Marketing On The Fun Side

People love to have fun, so why not provide it with your marketing techniques. Here are a few ways you can give it to them:

Run a contest- People will come from all over when a contest is announced. Run one on your blog or site to drive more traffic. You will have to market the contest pretty heavily to get people to hear about it, but once they know they will come running.

Make your contest fun that almost anyone can participate in. Offer a worthwhile prize to the winner of the contest. If you don't people won't come running the next time you run a contest or anything for your business.

A contest could be quizzes to take, an internet safari to participate in or just a raffle to draw names in.

Have Promotional products with your business logo- Websites like Cafe press will make products like T-shirts, pens, mugs and even hats with your logo on them. Some of these could be given away as gifts or you could have internet visitors purchase them through a link on your site.

These promotional items could be displayed so that anyone who comes in contact with that item will see your logo and be curious about whose business is on them. They can then search out your site to find out what exactly you offer.

Ending Thoughts

Anyone can run their own online business whether you have extensive business experience or not. All you really need is the drive to succeed and the ability to work hard and learn as much as you can about the business you choose to go into.

With the numerous options available for online businesses, you can find one that meets your needs and skills you have to bring to it. Use all the Marketing methods you can to get your business to reach all corners of the internet globe and drive traffic to your site.

The hard work and sweat you put into it initially will be worth it in the end as you can start to relax a little and maybe hire someone else to do some of your daily tasks for you. What better way to earn a living than to hire someone else to do your grunt work for you.

The internet brings more and more cash making opportunities to business owners every day, so why not get on the bandwagon now and start to reap some of the rewards that other internet marketers are achieving? If they can do it with little experience in the business field, so can you.

www.ingramcontent.com/pod-product-compliance
Lightning Source LLC
LaVergne TN
LVHW020742090526
838202LV00057BA/6189